Do You
KNOW
The Lord's Prayer?

Do You
KNOW
The Lord's Prayer?

P. Roose Lawson

Illustrated by Ed Roose

WestBow
P R E S S
A DIVISION OF THOMAS NELSON

WestBow Press books may be ordered through booksellers or by contacting:

WestBow Press
A Division of Thomas Nelson
1663 Liberty Drive
Bloomington, IN 47403
www.westbowpress.com
1-(866) 928-1240

Because of the dynamic nature of the Internet, any web addresses or links contained in
this book may have changed since publication and may no longer be valid. The views
expressed in this work are solely those of the author and do not necessarily reflect the
views of the publisher, and the publisher hereby disclaims any responsibility for them.

Any people depicted in stock imagery provided by Thinkstock are models,
and such images are being used for illustrative purposes only.

Certain stock imagery © Thinkstock.

ISBN: 978-1-4497-4418-2 (sc)
ISBN: 978-1-4497-4419-9 (e)

Library of Congress Control Number: 2012905099

Printed in the United States of America

WestBow Press rev. date: 4/12/2012

Dedication

To Madison and Michaela
who gave me the inspiration,
and - most especially - to
my FATHER.

P. Roose Lawson

"So what shall I do? I will pray with my spirit, but I will also pray with my understanding; I will sing with my spirit, but I will also sing with my understanding."

1 Corinthians 14:15 (N.I.V.)

Do You KNOW the Lord's Prayer?

To know the Lord's Prayer – to truly know it – takes more than memorization; it requires understanding, too. This book is offered to help with memorization as well as understanding.

We have printed The Lord's Prayer on every other page throughout this book to help you with memorization. Take the time to read it through each time it appears. Memorization involves repetition.

We have also given a line-by-line simple explanation of The Lord's Prayer so that you will better understand the words you are reading. As you read each explanation, stop to think about how it may apply to your life.

At the completion of this book, you will be able to say you do know The Lord's Prayer – not just as words that you repeat from memorization without even thinking, but with the spirit of understanding as well. You will know The Lord's Prayer—you will know it by heart!

THE LORD'S PRAYER

Our Father, who art in Heaven
hallowed be thy name.
Thy Kingdom come,
Thy will be done in earth as it is in Heaven.
Give us this day our daily bread
and forgive us our trespasses
as we forgive those who trespass against us.
And lead us not into temptation,
but deliver us from evil.
For Thine is the kingdom, and the power,
and the glory forever and ever.
Amen.

"The Lord's Prayer" - This prayer is sometimes referred to as "The Our Father". Guess we call it that because that's the first words of the prayer. Just so you know, it is called the Lord's Prayer because Jesus taught it to us. (We'll talk about that a bit later)

"Our Father who art in Heaven..."
We begin our prayer by declaring to God our understanding that He is our Father in Heaven. He's not like our earthly fathers – they can make mistakes and do wrong. Our God, our Heavenly Father, is the perfect example of what a father should be. He is our creator, our protector, our provider, our deliverer. Everything we have is from Him – the air in our lungs is His gift!

What a wonderful way to start our prayer – we let Him know that *we know* we are HIS!

Just so you know, the part where it says "who art in heaven..." the word 'art' is just an old English way of saying "who is in heaven" or "You are in heaven."

THE LORD'S PRAYER

Our Father, who art in Heaven
hallowed be thy name.
Thy Kingdom come,
Thy will be done in earth as it is in Heaven.
Give us this day our daily bread
and forgive us our trespasses
as we forgive those who trespass against us.
And lead us not into temptation,
but deliver us from evil.
For Thine is the kingdom, and the power,
and the glory forever and ever.
Amen.

"Hallowed" means

HONORED,
SACRED,
HOLY,
&
GREAT!

So, when we say "Hallowed be Your name" (or "thy name"), what we are saying is that we honor God so much that even His NAME is special to us. We bow down and humble ourselves at the sound of His name!

THE LORD'S PRAYER

Our Father, who art in Heaven
hallowed be thy name.
Thy Kingdom come,
Thy will be done in earth as it is in Heaven.
Give us this day our daily bread
and forgive us our trespasses
as we forgive those who trespass against us.
And lead us not into temptation,
but deliver us from evil.
For Thine is the kingdom, and the power,
and the glory forever and ever.
Amen.

"Kingdom come" – what does that mean??? Well, God is the greatest, best KING ever! He is the King of kings. Every king has a kingdom – "kingdoms" are empires or territories over which kings rule.

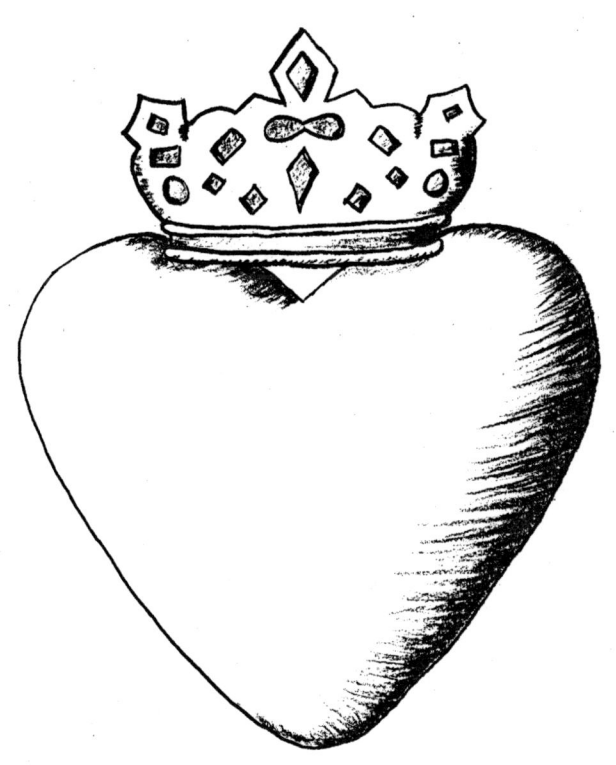

Our God rules over *everything* in heaven and *everything* in and on earth (and that includes us!). So, in this part of our prayer, we are inviting God to reign in our lives. We are saying to God, "Let us be a part of Your Kingdom - let Your kingdom <u>come to us</u> – let it come into our hearts so that we can be a part of it!"

YAY!

THE LORD'S PRAYER

Our Father, who art in Heaven
hallowed be thy name.
Thy Kingdom come,
**Thy will be done in earth as it is in
Heaven.**
Give us this day our daily bread
and forgive us our trespasses
as we forgive those who trespass against us.
And lead us not into temptation,
but deliver us from evil.
For Thine is the kingdom, and the power,
and the glory forever and ever.
Amen.

Here the word "will" is *not* like how we say, "I *will* go to the store" or "He *will* bring it to me." It is not that. Did you ever hear of someone having a will? We sometimes hear that someone is really sick, but they have a strong <u>will</u> to live. Or, there is also a document know as a <u>will</u> – as when someone dies and people read the will to see what the person wanted to have done with his possessions. Both the <u>will</u> to live and the <u>will</u> (document) are kind of the same. They both mean "want".

So, when we say to God, "Your will be done" we are saying that we want whatever He desires for us.

HIS WILL = HIS WANTS

We know that what we want (our will) is not always best; our will can get us into trouble, but God alone knows what is best for us – His <u>will</u> be done in our lives!

THE LORD'S PRAYER

Our Father, who art in Heaven
hallowed be thy name.
Thy Kingdom come,
Thy will be done in earth as it is in Heaven.
Give us this day our daily bread
and forgive us our trespasses
as we forgive those who trespass against us.
And lead us not into temptation,
but deliver us from evil.
For Thine is the kingdom, and the power,
and the glory forever and ever.
Amen.

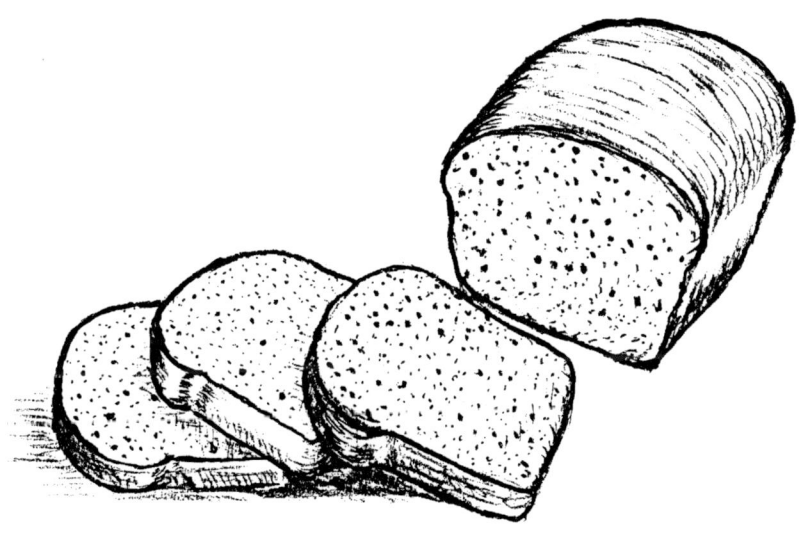

So what IS our "daily bread?" Notice the prayer doesn't say, "Give us this day our daily limousine ride," or "our daily steak and lobster with ice-cream for dessert." It says "our daily bread." Bread is seen as a basic – the food we need to survive, the air we breathe, the sip of refreshing water.

We don't ask God for extravagant gifts, we humbly ask Him to give us what we need to live *today* – the basics - nothing more, nothing less. By asking God for enough for this day, we let Him know that we depend on Him and trust Him to provide for us. We need only to be fed by the Bread of Life.

THE LORD'S PRAYER

Our Father, who art in Heaven
hallowed be thy name.
Thy Kingdom come,
Thy will be done in earth as it is in Heaven.
Give us this day our daily bread
and forgive us our trespasses
as we forgive those who trespass against us.
And lead us not into temptation,
but deliver us from evil.
For Thine is the kingdom, and the power,
and the glory forever and ever.
Amen.

"Forgive us our trespasses" is an odd phrase, but if we think about what it is to trespass on someone's property, it means we have crossed a line – we have done something wrong, we have gone where we should not be going.

God has given us rules to live by – commandments – that are really and truly for our own good, but many times we 'cross the lines' He has given us. Here we are saying, "Forgive me, Father God, when I have crossed that line. Forgive me when I have trespassed and offended You or another human being." (Just ask and He will forgive you!)

NOTE: Many versions of the Lord's Prayer use the words, "forgive us our debts as we also have forgiven our debtors." Some other versions say, "forgive us our sins as we have forgiven those who sin against us." The words: 'trespass,' 'debt,' and 'sin' have something in common. All of them mean that we have crossed a line, owe an apology, or have done something wrong against God or against another person. Whatever the words used, we ask God to forgive us so we can start over, fresh and new - freed from our sin.

THE LORD'S PRAYER

Our Father, who art in Heaven
hallowed be thy name.
Thy Kingdom come,
Thy will be done in earth as it is in Heaven.
Give us this day our daily bread
and forgive us our trespasses
as we forgive those who trespass against us.
And lead us not into temptation,
but deliver us from evil.
For Thine is the kingdom, and the power,
and the glory forever and ever.
Amen.

It stands to reason that at some point in our lives, someone is going to 'cross the line' with us. They have done something wrong to us. They have trespassed against us – offended us in some way – and, in our mind, they owe us an apology. Will we forgive them?

If we are bold enough to ask God to forgive us when WE are the ones who do wrong, then we know in our hearts – and by the Word of our Lord – that we also must forgive others when they do wrong against us. How can we ask for forgiveness from God Almighty for our sins if we do not forgive others?

GOD DOESN'T HAVE DOUBLE STANDARDS!

THE LORD'S PRAYER

Our Father, who art in Heaven
hallowed be thy name.
Thy Kingdom come,
Thy will be done in earth as it is in Heaven.
Give us this day our daily bread
and forgive us our trespasses
as we forgive those who trespass against us.
And lead us not into temptation,
but deliver us from evil.
For Thine is the kingdom, and the power,
and the glory forever and ever.
Amen.

Here we ask God to help us in times of temptation. Temptation is everywhere around us. We are tempted in so many ways each and every day. We sometimes want to spread rumors about others, even though we know it is best for us to keep silent. We see things on the internet, television, advertising or in movies that we know we should not be seeing, but we are so tempted to keep looking. We hear music delivered by various media that is not designed for the ears of a child of God, yet, we want to listen more.

By giving in (caving!) to these types of temptations, we are trespassing. So, here, we ask God to help us 'not even go there.' We ask for His help to keep us away from that temptation. When we put God first in our lives, we find it easier to follow His ways.

THE LORD'S PRAYER

Our Father, who art in Heaven
hallowed be thy name.
Thy Kingdom come,
Thy will be done in earth as it is in Heaven.
Give us this day our daily bread
and forgive us our trespasses
as we forgive those who trespass against us.
And lead us not into temptation,
but deliver us from evil.
For Thine is the kingdom, and the power,
and the glory forever and ever.
Amen.

In this part of the sentence, the word "but" can be substituted with the word "instead." That way we are saying to God: "Don't lead us into temptation, <u>instead</u> deliver us from evil."

And now we get to the words "deliver us." That is another odd phrase for us to use. To help figure this out, we can ask ourselves, "What does it mean to 'deliver' something?" Well, it means to take something from one place to another.

What is evil? Evil is anything that is against God. Evil is sin. Evil is Satan. Evil is turning our backs on God and doing what WE want to do instead of what HE wants us to do.

So, when we ask God to "deliver us from evil," we are actually asking Him, "Please, God, get us out of here! Get us away from things that are not of YOU. Speak to our hearts, turn us around and head us in the right direction!"

God is our Deliverer! He will help us out of bad situations if we listen to Him!

THE LORD'S PRAYER

Our Father, who art in Heaven
hallowed be thy name.
Thy Kingdom come,
Thy will be done in earth as it is in Heaven.
Give us this day our daily bread
and forgive us our trespasses
as we forgive those who trespass against us.
And lead us not into temptation,
but deliver us from evil.
***For Thine is the kingdom, and the
power, and the glory forever and ever.**
Amen.

The word 'Thine' means 'Yours.'

This last sentence of our prayer is saying, "Yours is the Kingdom, Yours is the power, Yours is the glory forever." We are again saying to God that we know He is the Almighty, He is all powerful, He is all glorious, all honorable and all holy – He is OUR GOD for now and to the end of time!

GOD LOVES TO HEAR OUR PRAISE!

*NOTE: Without getting real technical, it should probably be explained that not all versions of the Lord's Prayer contain this final sentence – but many do! Bible scholars - even to this day - debate whether or not it was included in the original text of the Bible. Whether it was or was not, it is still a beautiful doxology – or short hymn of praise – that is at the end of the prayer.

THE LORD'S PRAYER

Our Father, who art in Heaven
hallowed be thy name.
Thy Kingdom come,
Thy will be done in earth as it is in Heaven.
Give us this day our daily bread
and forgive us our trespasses
as we forgive those who trespass against us.
And lead us not into temptation,
but deliver us from evil.
For Thine is the kingdom, and the power,
and the glory forever and ever.

Amen.

We end nearly all our prayers with the word, "Amen." It is a single word sentence. Do you know what it means? We are not saying, "the end," we are not saying, "goodbye". What we are actually saying is something more like, "So be it" or "Truly" or in more modern terms, we are simply saying, "Yes." We are saying that we confirm all that we said in the prayer to be true. It is like adding our personal, verbal signature to the prayer we have just recited.

SO NOW...

Before we once more read the whole prayer through, it is good to know the origin of the prayer. As Christians, we recite the prayer often, but where did it originate?

In the Bible, in the book called "Matthew," in the sixth chapter, it is written that Jesus said, "This, then, is how you should pray...." and He then spoke the words of this prayer – that is why we call it 'The Lord's Prayer.' It was given to us by our Lord, Jesus Christ, as instructions on _how to pray_.

The Lord's Prayer = How to Pray

We can recite the Lord's Prayer as it is written, for it is indeed the perfect prayer. We can also use it as a format (or sample) for any prayer we offer to God. When we use it as a model, we can see that we should:

1. Always begin with praise for God, acknowledging that He is God, the Creator King who rules over everything. We lift our hands and raise our head, or we bow down in humbleness – either way we praise His holy name!

2. We remember that whatever is in God's vast and mighty plan, it is the best for us. His will, not ours.

3. Next, we ask our Father God for that which is good for us for today. This is the part - in any prayer we offer - where we ask for our needs. Sometimes our needs are great and sometimes they are simple, so we merely ask for whatever makes up "our daily bread" for today.

4. We also need to include the confession of (owning up to) our sins. Because of what Jesus did for us, we need only to be truly sorry for our 'trespassings' as we ask for forgiveness and our loving Father God will 'wipe us clean' from our wrongdoings. By His loving grace, He forgives us. Then we can turn away from our old ways and begin fresh and new. (Don't forget – we need to give the gift of forgiveness to others as well!)

5. Then, we tell God – in whatever words we have for Him – that we will follow His lead. When we find ourselves in times of trouble, we know that if we ask Him, He will 'deliver' us to comfort.

6. Finally, in the same way as we start our prayers, we should finish with praise and honor for our God. He is our King! He is all powerful! He is all glorious from now until the end of time!

7. Amen. So be it. I believe these words to be true and I verbally sign my name to this prayer.

So, here it is, The Lord's Prayer,

one more time for our review with (hopefully) a little better understanding.......

THE LORD'S PRAYER

Our Father, who art in Heaven
hallowed be thy name.
Thy Kingdom come,
Thy will be done in earth as it is in Heaven.
Give us this day our daily bread
and forgive us our trespasses
as we forgive those who trespass against us.
And lead us not into temptation,
but deliver us from evil.
For Thine is the kingdom, and the power,
and the glory forever and ever.
Amen.

NOTES

NOTES

NOTES

NOTES

CPSIA information can be obtained at www.ICGtesting.com
Printed in the USA
BVOW012059020512

289237BV00005B/32/P